Successful Net
In A Week

Alison Straw and Dena Michelli

Alison Straw is an independent consultant and executive coach. Her career has been devoted to helping individuals, groups and organizations develop. She is passionate about engaging and inspiring people and has worked with many senior executives, supporting them in developing themselves, their careers and their organizations.

Dena Michelli is an executive coach and leadership development specialist who works across cultures in business school and organizational settings. She is particularly interested in how people move through transition and change and undertook research to map this process for her PhD.

Teach® Yourself

Successful Networking

Alison Straw
and
Dena Michelli

IN A WEEK

www.inaweek.co.uk

Hodder Education

338 Euston Road, London NW1 3BH.

Hodder Education is an Hachette UK company

First published in UK 1995 by Hodder Education

First published in US 2012 by The McGraw-Hill Companies, Inc.

This edition published 2012

British Library Cataloguing in Publication Data: a catalogue record for this title is available from the British Library.

Library of Congress Catalog Card Number: on file.

10 9 8 7 6 5 4 3 2

The publisher has used its best endeavours to ensure that any website addresses referred to in this book are correct and active at the time of going to press. However, the publisher and the author have no responsibility for the websites and can make no guarantee that a site will remain live or that the content will remain relevant, decent or appropriate.

The publisher has made every effort to mark as such all words which it believes to be trademarks. The publisher should also like to make it clear that the presence of a word in the book, whether marked or unmarked, in no way affects its legal status as a trademark.

Every reasonable effort has been made by the publisher to trace the copyright holders of material in this book. Any errors or omissions should be notified in writing to the publisher, who will endeavour to rectify the situation for any reprints and future editions.

Hachette UK's policy is to use papers that are natural, renewable and recyclable products and made from wood grown in sustainable forests. The logging and manufacturing processes are expected to conform to the environmental regulations of the country of origin.

www.hoddereducation.co.uk

Typeset by Cenveo Publisher Services.

Printed in Great Britain by CPI Group (UK) Ltd, Croydon, CR0 4YY.

Contents

Introduction

Networking is a word that is firmly embedded in our vocabulary. It is not unusual to hear the word used to describe a range of activities and behaviours.

The **activities** of a successful networker are often focussed on outcomes. Our research and observations suggest that successful networkers build their networks by developing close relationships with work colleagues, professional communities and associations and virtually, through social and professional networking sites, referrals and references from friends or colleagues.

The **behaviours** of a successful networker are often social. Successful networkers may be considered to be gregarious; when you observe them, it becomes clear they build relationships through empathic connections, being respectful, purposeful and reciprocal relationships that are founded on principles such as 'do as you would be done by'.

Individuals respond to the word **network** in different ways. While researching this book, we talked to many people and found diametrically opposed views. At one extreme, there were those who were vehemently opposed to networking:

I wouldn't dream of using people in such a manipulative way!

I hate asking for favours!

I dread going when the invitation says it's a networking event!

At the other end of the extreme, we found strong believers in networking who enjoyed the benefits of their well-developed network:

I couldn't exist without it!

Professionally and personally, it's a lifesaver!

I've been given opportunities that I would have missed otherwise!

However you respond to the word, networks can make the difference for you personally and professionally. *Successful Networking* is designed to help you understand, benefit from and develop your network.

SUNDAY

Networks and networking

Traditionally, organizations were structured as relatively self-contained units and those who operated within them were assigned clearly defined roles. This level of structure, definition and order meant that most internal processes were routine and the channels of communication were well mapped. Today, organizations are very different. Hierarchy and 'chains of command' have been replaced by fluid, organic arrangements in a global context that can respond rapidly to the needs of the market.

Jobs at all levels of any organization are no longer defined by a set of impersonal and technical tasks. Managers' performance is judged on their ability to deliver, adapt and add value by being creative and 'fleet of foot'. Their success will be dependent upon their understanding of the relationships that exist inside and outside the organization and their ability to invest in them using their networking skills.

Building and managing your network is not only your key to organizational success, it supports and nourishes you personally. However, as a concept, networking is in need of demystifying. Let's look first at the *Webster's Dictionary* definition:

n. 'A fabric or structure of cords or wires that cross at regular intervals and are knotted or secured at the crossings'

v. 'To make connections among people or groups'

What you require from your network will undoubtedly vary. Your networking goals may be formal and structured, such as meeting peers and asking for their advice on how to achieve your career goals. Or they may be informal and unstructured, such as contacting a friend and saying: 'Am I going crazy? You'll never believe what happened to me today!' Or semi-formal and structured, such as the social networking sites that have proliferated on the Internet.

Networking is not a precise science, nor is it an entirely tangible range of activities and behaviours. To help you understand networking, we are going to give you a framework that focuses on the benefits and types of networks. This chapter gives the following overview:

- Networks:
  - Network types
  - Network relationships
  - Networks? What networks?!
- Networking:
  - Networking styles.

Networks

If you were to take a bird's-eye view of your life and focus on your relationships and networks, it would soon become clear that they are both complex and dynamic. Networks spring from different sources; they are established in different environments and serve different purposes.

Network types

Your relationships evolve mainly through associations. These may have developed through a variety of circumstances, such as attending the same school or college, living in the same area or working in the same organization. Or they may have evolved through your interests, your desire to be in regular contact with people you know, or your wish to meet new people.

We have identified four basic types of network:

- personal
- organizational
- professional
- social.

The relationships we establish through these networks are active and reciprocal – and their boundaries are sometimes blurred. For example, relationships initially established through working together (your organizational network) often progress to friendships and, as such, become part of your personal or social network – where your engagement and expectations are different.

Personal networks

These include: friends, family and acquaintances or 'friends' you have made on the social networking sites. Whether they are face-to-face or virtual, personal networks often emerge around a school, college, church, sports club, shared interest or activity. Generally, you choose your personal networks based upon liking, reciprocity, mutual connections or interests. Personal networks tend to be social; they are usually developed outside the working environment and are based upon an exchange of help and support.

Organizational networks

The range of social, cultural and technological processes that have existed in the more traditional, hierarchical, organizations are now breaking down, resulting in devolution of power and responsibility. This promotes sharing information and co-working in order to pursue common objectives, solve problems and satisfy the expectations and needs of internal and external stakeholders.

Team and project work are now common in today's organizations. They don't have the restrictions of departments, divisions, culture, locality or hierarchy. Teams, project groups, committees and councils all provide ideal conditions for networking. When you put together a team or become part of a project, you've assembled a vast and powerful network.

These networks are normally focussed and developed on the basis of who you need to know in order to meet your objective within a particular timescale. They are not necessarily based on status, but on knowledge, skills and influence. A key strategy, when joining a new department, division or organization is to identify the organizational network as soon as possible, and in particular, those with overt and covert power.

Professional networks

Professional networks are normally made up of associates, colleagues, suppliers and clients. Professional networks are built around common work interests and tasks. They can be formal networks to which you affiliate, such as institutes, societies, alumni groups and professional associations. Or they can be more fluid and exploratory, such as those held on LinkedIn®. They can also be less formal, such as a voluntary group that comes together over a set of values or a charitable cause.

Whereas a personal network is determined by whom you like, a professional network is created around knowledge and circumstances. Your professional networks will no doubt change over time. You may, for example, join an organization that reflects your technical speciality at the beginning of your career. As your career develops, you may join other organizations that reflect your changing responsibilities, aspirations and interests. You may also be invited to participate in executive or non-executive roles that place you in a wider professional, and perhaps more diverse, network.

Social networks

The opportunity to make personal connections of global scope is now only one click away. Social networks – now too many to name – have enjoyed exponential growth and many of them count their members by tens, if not hundreds, of millions. The blessing and the curse of this phenomenon is access to people you would probably never have encountered in your everyday life – a blessing because the social and cultural barriers have almost completely dissolved, a curse because it is difficult to manage the myriad 'friends' and the flow of information that stems from them. Increased exposure and visibility are two of the outcomes of social networking, again, bringing both advantages and disadvantages. If you seek notoriety, it is there for the taking. If you seek privacy, you may be disappointed.

Network relationships

Regardless of the type of network in which you operate, you will be forming relationships for different reasons. The most basic reason is need. We are social creatures by nature and need the approval and feedback provided by those with whom we relate. Not only this, but also we need the more practical assistance and guidance that our network can offer us. You will no doubt benefit from your networks in different ways:

Networks provide:

- information
- development
- support
- influence.

Information

Every manager needs information for gaining new perspectives. Information in the form of data on trends, markets and opportunities facilitate sound planning. Information is not solely about the future; being well-informed means that you can tackle situations before they occur, anticipate problems and manage tricky situations. Our action can also be influenced by information on options, strategies and possible solutions.

Development

Managers are confronted by an ever-changing environment. For this reason, they need to be constantly developing their skills and behaviours. Development can take many forms. Traditionally, training was the route to development but today there are many other forms of development at our disposal. Coaching and mentoring have gained popularity as a time and money efficient approach to targeted development.

Support

Our well-being depends on feeling supported. Perhaps we only recognize its importance when it is removed. Support can be as simple as someone showing an interest, being there or offering guidance or practical help.

Influence

Networks can give you access to resources and political muscle. In the short term, these are clearly important to your success. However, these networks can also be important to your long-term future. Identifying key people, who can open doors, sponsor and be an advocate for you can make a real difference to your career.

Defining these categories of networks should provide you with the framework you require to look objectively at yours and make the necessary judgements about how to build and manage them. The key to successful networking is balance. We have heard managers say:

'All my energy has been concentrated on work. I'm not sure if I still have any friends!'

'I seem to spend all my time supporting others. Who's supporting me?!'

Many people concentrate their efforts on organizational networks to the detriment of their personal networks. Or the relationships in their networks become one-sided. Many networks have evolved rather than been planned and, as a result, they can become unbalanced and demanding. Networks need monitoring and reviewing to ensure that they are still serving their purpose and are beneficial to all members.

Networks? What networks?!

Networks do not exist by magic. They develop as a result of an investment of time and energy. Unfortunately, investment in one area can result in a lack of investment in another. Think about the kind of relationships you have in your networks. Do you currently have restricted access to information, development, support or influence? If so, what adjustments would benefit you?

Networks evolve over time; they change shape and size according to your interests and circumstances. Ask yourself the following questions:

What do I want from my network?
Is my network serving me?
How could my network work better for me?

It is important to ask yourself these key questions regularly. If you are clear about what you want, you can be precise in your networking.

Networking

The benefits of establishing and maintaining effective relationships are well documented. Most people recognize that relationships are vitally important in all areas of life. Your personal happiness, satisfaction and your physical well-being depend on the quality of your relationships. Networking is all about relationships!

Before we move on, try answering the following questions. Do you:

- usually accept opportunities to meet new people?
- have contacts in a wide variety of groups?
- feel that you're generally well informed?
- share information with those around you?
- stay in close contact with your customers or clients?
- regularly attend meetings, training courses and conferences?
- know and talk to peers in other organizations?

If you answered no to any of the above, think about the reasons why. What prevents you?

To be successful at networking, you need to have an interest in building relationships and create opportunities for doing so.

This can be achieved by adopting different styles. You may recognize your style from the following model.

Networking styles

When you start on any journey, you have choices. You will choose your means of transportation, your preferred route and your schedule. Networking is like planning a journey. First, you have to be clear about your destination and then you have to make your choices. These will depend upon:

● the time available
● how specific your destination is.

You also have choices regarding your style of networking.
   The main styles of networking are:

● targeted
● intuitive
● open.

Targeted
Targeted networkers recognize the gaps in their networks. They identify opportunities to exploit and people to fill the gaps. This style is often used by those seeking career development and for creating purposeful alliances.

Intuitive
Intuitive networkers are natural catalysts and enablers. Their relationships are based on mutuality and are prompted by common needs or values. Naturally, they develop strong and wide networks. However, the focus for all their networks tends to be altruistic, and sometimes intuitive networkers have trouble translating their networks into something that can benefit them.

Open
Open networkers tend to travel in a defined direction. They invest in networks for their future potential. They develop new networks to match their interests and careers.
   So, what's your natural networking style?

Summary

We began today by proposing that networks and networking could be the key to your personal happiness and professional success. If your continued happiness and success are important to you, we suggest that you take this proposition seriously. Networking is not a miracle cure or a fad. Networks are all around us. It is how we use and benefit from them that can make all the difference to our futures.

Take the time to understand:

Your networks

● Types
- Personal
- Organizational
- Professional
- Social
● Benefits
- Information
- Development
- Support
- Influence
● Your networking style
- Targeted
- Intuitive
- Open

Challenge yourself with these questions:
● *How has my network developed?*
● *What does my network look like?*
● *How comfortable do I feel with networking?*
● *What is my style?*
● *What do I want from my network?*
● *How could I network more effectively?*
● *What do I need to do differently?*

In each chapter, we'll build on your responses to these questions.

SUNDAY

MONDAY

TUESDAY

WEDNESDAY

THURSDAY

FRIDAY

SATURDAY

Questions

Answer the following questions honestly, reflecting on your approach to networking:

1. **What do you believe is the purpose of networking?**
   a) To build a dynamic community ❑
   b) To assist others get what they want ❑
   c) To get what you want ❑
   d) To give you the upper hand ❑

2. **How do you feel about your networking abilities?**
   a) I use my network when I need assistance ❑
   b) To build 'credit' in my network by helping others ❑
   c) I avoid asking others for help ❑
   d) I think networking is manipulative and I dislike it ❑

3. **What is your preferred style of networking?**
   a) Conscious ❑
   b) Intuitive ❑
   c) Open ❑
   d) I don't network ❑

4. **How often do you access your network?**
   a) 1–2 day ❑
   b) 1–2 week ❑
   c) 1–2 month ❑
   d) Hardly ever ❑

5. **What kind of networks do you build?**
   a) Personal ❑
   b) Organizational ❑
   c) Professional ❑
   d) Social ❑

6. **Primarily, what do you use your networks for?**
   a) Information ❑
   b) Development ❑
   c) Support ❑
   d) Influence ❑

7. **Reflecting on your network, what has been the most useful/helpful outcome?**
   a) A new role or organization ❑
   b) Essential commercial information ❑
   c) I have built some important personal/business relationships ❑
   d) I have had fun ❑

8. **What does your network look like?**
   a) It is diverse ❑
   b) It is focussed on my profession/specialism/role ❑
   c) It is predominantly social
   d) It is based around my interests ❑

9. **How could you network more effectively?**
a) I could be more proactive ❏
b) Being more effective would be challenging ❏
c) I could seek new networks ❏
d) I could regularly communicate with my network ❏

10. **How do you manage your network?**
a) I prune contacts that I no longer need ❏
b) My network manages me ❏
c) I communicate with each person regularly ❏
d) I invite new members to join my network ❏

MONDAY

Personal networks

You are born into a network. Personal networks are central to your early development: supporting, teaching and guiding you. As you grow older, some of these functions are replaced by institutions, organizations or significant others – and the importance of your family network changes.

You never lose your need for personal networks and, as you mature, they remain as important to your well-being as they ever were in your formative years. You may, however, become focussed on other networks. We have often heard managers admit that their personal networks are small compared to their professional networks. Indeed, they may be solely focussed on their nuclear family and a few friends. This happens mainly because they have spent time putting emphasis on their professional networks to the detriment of those in their close circle.

Personal networks are usually based on mutuality and liking. You meet many people throughout your life but only a few of these would be classified as friends and allowed into your personal network. You can gauge eligibility using a number of indicators. Personal networks are made up of those whom you:

● choose to spend time with
● invite to your home
● miss, if deprived of their company.

Think for a moment about your personal network.

Personal networks need investment, development, nurturing and commitment. This is not a simple task. It can be more challenging to develop a personal network than any professional or organizational network because you have to build the structure. It is easy to take the goodwill of those in our personal network for granted. Being as conscious of these people as we are of those in our professional network is very important. We will begin by identifying methods to help you.

This chapter discusses:

● Recognizing personal networks
● Developing networks
● Nurturing networks

Recognizing personal networks

There are many personal networks at your disposal.

Education

When we mention personal networks established through education, we are not only talking about old school friends. Your school ties may have remained strong, but many find they have little in common with school friends beyond their shared experience at school. It is more likely that the personal

relationships you established in your later educational career will stand the test of time. The strength of these networks is often based upon an interest in a specific subject, entry into a similar profession or on shared formative memories.

Work

We meet many people through work, including:

- bosses
- colleagues
- peers
- subordinates
- suppliers
- customers.

The proximity of working relationships and the time you spend at work creates an environment in which close friendships and partnerships can develop. Other networks develop through extracurricular activities such as a social club, health club, interest groups, commuting together, or something as informal as a drink after work.

The personal networks established though work can be powerful.

Leisure

As you develop interests, you will build different networks.
Leisure networks could be built around:

- sport and fitness
- interests
- hobbies
- voluntary work
- causes.

Shared interests and a common commitment bring you together with people in leisure networks. The reason for meeting can become less important than the meeting itself as these networks develop. Golf clubs, health clubs, sports teams, volunteering, interests, night school and political or cause-related groups provide excellent opportunities for networking.

Family

It is likely that you will be influenced most strongly by your family network and how it functions. Your perspective on networks and networking will be determined by this experience. Your family networks include the nuclear family, the extended family and family friends.

One of the positive facets of a family network is that members generally have high regard for each other – or at least, loyalty towards each other! For the purposes of its survival, if nothing else, a family tends to have each other's well-being at heart. Referrals from family members can sometimes be the strongest and often result in really valuable opportunities.

Personal networks are not entities that just happen. As with other networks, they can be developed to match your needs at critical points in your life.

All of your existing networks have peripheral networks attached to them. If you are clear about what you want from your personal network, you are likely to be able to access it and its extended network and develop both 'first tier' and 'second tier' relationships to help you meet your life goals.

Think about your personal network:

- *What peripheral networks are attached to your personal networks?*
- *Where are the gaps in your network?*
- *How would you like your personal networks to develop?*
- *How can you develop them?*

What you may be seeking through your personal networks are opportunities to meet with like-minded people in a non-work environment. Be clear about your needs and goals in establishing personal networks. Personal networks can provide opportunities for:

- support
- stimulation
- challenge
- appreciation
- acceptance
- involvement
- enjoyment.

A simple gauge to help you identify your needs is balance. It is as important to have balanced relationships as it is to develop the right personal network to reflect your needs.

So how do you develop these relationships?

Developing networks

Personal networks exist all around you. Although, for many, these remain untapped resources, they can serve many functions and develop in all sorts of ways. You establish personal networks by:

- keeping in touch
- taking initiatives
- building bridges
- communicating proactively
- cultivating contacts
- offering assistance.

This doesn't mean being pushy. First, identify the gap between your network and your needs. Think about who could help you enter other networks that could fill the gaps and bring you value. Then start talking, meeting and building your network.

Nurturing networks

Networks are sensitive. If you feed networks and look after them with care and attention, you will reap the rewards.
   In order to nurture networks:

- be open-minded
- keep commitments
- treat others as you would like to be treated
- don't be afraid to ask
- give without exception or expectation
- recognize problems and address them
- say 'thank you' – in word and/or in deed.

Be open-minded

Being open-minded is the golden rule of networking. If you close your mind to the concept or the principle of networking, your efforts are likely to fail. Enter new situations with a degree of optimism about the people you'll meet and their role in your future.

Try to treat those you dislike as respectfully as those you favour. They may have just as much to offer. Often, what you dislike in others is a reflection of what you dislike in yourself. So try not to judge others and be generous and accepting of them.

Keep commitments

When you make a commitment to do something for someone else, you can never be sure of its importance or value to them. People tend to build their hopes around promises and commitments. By cultivating the habit of always keeping commitments and being reliable, you can build relationships on the basis of trust and credibility that can span the gaps in your network and generate warmth, good will and reciprocity.

Treat others as you would like to be treated

Standards and expectations are important in building relationships.

Ask yourself: *How would I like to be treated?*

Be honest in developing relationships. Only nurture those that you are prepared to invest in. Otherwise, it can seem that you discard people callously when they have served their purpose. Personal integrity generates trust.

You will be noticed by others and you will gain a reputation – for good or bad!

Don't be afraid to ask

Dependency is a value-laden term. To be told that you are dependent smacks of an insult in a society like ours that values independence. However, the notion of 'true' independence is misconceived. People are not utterly self-sufficient. We all need relationships to perform our work effectively and to live happy and fulfilled lives – interdependency seems to us a much better description.

Many managers have strong networks but they often lack the ability to benefit from them personally and professionally.

Give without exception or expectation

Anthropologists tell us that exchanges, assistance and giving are the most common functions of friendships in all cultures. Giving is one of the basic rules of networking.

People help each other in different ways for different reasons. This is why it can be difficult to network with those you have little in common with or even dislike. The type of help you offer is not particularly important. The fact that you are prepared to give is what counts.

A level of altruism is required to be a successful networker. You should not give with the expectation that you'll receive something in return. You will benefit at some stage in your relationship but if you make this the only reason for networking, you may be disappointed. Be careful of giving excessively. An effusive networker can be a real turn-off.

Recognize problems

It may seem harsh to speak of relationships, and particularly those within your personal network, as effective or ineffective. However, it is vital to assess your relationships in this way when considering your network.

Personal networks need to stay effective. They often begin this way and it is likely that this is why they formed in the first place. But they can be corrupted by changes in circumstances, such as others coming into the network or the rationale for the existence of your network changing, such as a change in your goals and aspirations.

By investing in some relationships, you can change them from being ineffective to effective. The strength of the tie may determine whether you choose to invest in the relationship or not. You may decide, simply, to distance yourself from ineffective relationships in recognition that they will not change.

Be sure to act when you recognize a problem in your network. By careful and regular monitoring, you can ensure that relationship issues rarely occur.

Say thank you

If someone is helping you, let them know how much you appreciate it. If you take the time to say or do something to show your appreciation, it will create an ongoing dynamic of assistance. Personal networks are often the most sensitive. You can express your appreciation in a variety of ways. Send them a newspaper clipping, an article, details of a seminar, meeting or social event. Very little effort is required to create a feeling of concern and belonging.

Summary

Personal networks are easy to overlook because they are almost like 'second nature' to us.

The pressing needs of our busy lives can create situations where we neglect the relationships that we benefit from the most.

Yet personal networks can deliver immense value if we care to nurture them and use them with care and consideration. Think about how many years of experience is collectively held by the members of your personal network. There will be those who have had successful careers, those who have started new businesses, those who have made a social impact in their local community and those who have a global network that will keep you alert and attuned to different behavioural rhythms.

Take time to review and invest in your personal network. This means thinking about who your personal network contains, the expectations you have of each other and identifying the gaps between your goals and aspirations and what your network can deliver. Ensure that you 'do unto others as you would be done to' and consider what proactive steps would build and maintain the goodwill in your network.

Your personal network contains people who have known you the longest and have seen you in all your personal and career incarnations. As a result of their long-term perspective, the members of your personal network hold valuable insights into your talents and potential. Their words may be challenging, but they are often wise. Overlook your personal network at your peril!

SUNDAY

MONDAY

TUESDAY

WEDNESDAY

THURSDAY

FRIDAY

SATURDAY

Questions

Answer the following questions honestly, reflecting on the nature of the relationships within your network.

1. **How often do you review your personal network?**
   a) Daily–weekly ☐
   b) Monthly–yearly ☐
   c) Less than every two years ☐
   d) Never ☐

2. **What is your attitude when meeting new people?**
   a) I love to meet new people ☐
   b) I'm shy of meeting people ☐
   c) I force myself to network when I think it's important ☐
   d) I dread meeting new people ☐

3. **How often do you use your personal network to make contacts?**
   a) My personal network is my 'first stop' ☐
   b) My personal network is social ☐
   c) I rarely look to my personal network ☐
   d) I never think of my personal network ☐

4. **How effective is your personal network?**
   a) Members of my personal network deliver value ☐
   b) My network contains some valuable relationships ☐
   c) My network is very patchy ☐
   d) My personal network doesn't serve me at all ☐

5. **How could you build your personal network?**
   a) I need to invest time nurturing relationships ☐
   b) I need to be proactive in building my network ☐
   c) I need to rid my network of redundant members ☐
   d) It serves its purpose ☐

6. **What will you do to build and sustain your personal network?**
   a) I will attend more events at which I can network ☐
   b) I will access new networks through the members of my own ☐
   c) I am focussing on my professional network ☐
   d) I will think about what I can do for others in my network ☐

7. **How do you select the members of your personal network?**
   a) I invite people I like to join my network ☐
   b) I see who is active in other people's networks ☐
   c) I wait for people to build relationships with me ☐
   d) I wait until I have a need ☐

8. How do you nurture your network?

a) I make sure I speak to everyone regularly ❏

b) I invite people to come with me to events ❏

c) I regularly send articles, papers or other things of interest ❏

d) I wait to be asked ❏

9. When you have a particular need, how do you meet it through your network?

a) I approach people and ask for help directly ❏

b) I find an opportunity to get together ❏

c) I ask what I can do for them ❏

d) I drop hints that I need help and hope that they offer ❏

10. How do you use your network to leverage your reputation?

a) I ask to join others at events ❏

b) I ask for feedback on my impact on others ❏

c) I make myself known make myself known to a wider audience ❏

d) I look to my organizational network for my reputation ❏

TUESDAY

Organizational networks

Traditionally, organizations were founded on the principles of hierarchy, systems and structures. They were, by character, inflexible and bureaucratic with prescribed ways to approach tasks that now seem time-consuming and clumsy.

This is only part of the picture. On closer inspection, under the formal façade, you would discover an informal power base. People were and are the power holders in organizations. These people are the hubs of your organizational network. You are probably intuitively aware of who they are. You may or may not like them very much.

Who are the hubs within your organization?

Hubs can:

- Inform
  - What's going on?
  - How would this be seen?
- Influence
  - Who should I talk to?
  - How should I present myself and my ideas?
- Get things done
  - What are the shortcuts?
  - Are there 'hidden' rules?

Hubs are not necessarily those people with the longest service, highest status or the outward exhibition of power. They are more likely to be natural networkers.

When you enter any new environment, it is worth identifying the hubs. Don't do this rashly – first impressions can be misleading. Consider carefully where the informal information and power lies. These centres of information and power can be identified by making some of the following observations.

Who:

● eats together and socializes (friends)?
● provides solutions (experts)?
● are the sources of 'sensitive' information (moles)?
● receives the resources (support)?
● is in the right place at the right time (guides)?

The traditional organizations we have discussed are changing. Generally speaking, hierarchies are being replaced by democracies and status is being replaced by relationships as the basis of power.

To be successful within any organizational culture, you need to understand the principles of networking and recognize the power of relationships. It is these organizational networks that we will be focussing upon in this chapter:

● Organizational structures
● The 'network principle'
● Inter-organizational networks

Organizational structures

Just as physical structures are designed for a specific purpose or effect – rockers on rocking chairs enabling them to rock, wheels on wheelbarrows enabling them to roll – organizational structures can be, and are, designed for a specific purpose or effect.

Organizational structures are typically defined by production processes or service provision. They have characteristics that reflect different sectors, people, history, ownership, culture... The list is endless. We have chosen three common, yet different, structures for contrast:

● flat organizations
● hierarchical organizations
● networked organizations.

Flat organizations

As a result of economic difficulties, many organizations have stripped out layers of management. This has been necessary to meet the competitive market challenges and withstand the pressures of the troubled global economy.

As a result, a high value has been placed on managers who not only have a functional speciality, but also have diverse experience and understand the business drivers. To complement this experience, knowledge and understanding, organizations value managers with interpersonal and communications skills. These are people who can demonstrate leadership capabilities on projects and with teams and who have the ability to communicate effectively across various departments and business units.

Hierarchical organizations

These organizations have the traditional, pyramid style of organization. They usually have a chairperson and chief executive officer at the apex of the pyramid and multiple layers of management, which increase in number as they descend to the bottom of the pyramid where the 'real' work is done!

The method of communication in these organizations is strictly controlled. It is usually vertical (up and down the organization) and can become blocked very easily if someone chooses to withhold information or a decision.

Hierarchical structures encourage specialities. Managers tend to focus on the small, rather than the big picture, with limited insights across their functional borders. It can create an environment of divisions – or silos – which makes it difficult for the organization to advance as an integrated 'whole'.

Networked organizations

The new and emerging organizations of today are often based upon the 'network principle'. They have changed their structure and their styles of communication to enhance their efficiency and performance. Networked (or matrix) organizations aim to combine the best of hierarchical vision and control with a cross-functional, project-based approach.

These three organizational structures are compared in the table below:

	Flat	Hierarchical	Networked
Communication	Horizontal Without boundaries Between peers	Vertical Pre-defined channels Within functional groups	Vertical/ Horizontal Broad communication encouraged Focussed on projects/ outcomes
Innovation	Flourishes Practical problems resolved	Can be lost in the hierarchy Progress can be slow until 'go' decision made	Emergent and supported Implemented through project teams
Information	Fluid Information readily circulated	Through specific/ formal channels Information protected and sometimes withheld	No formal boundaries Focussed on purpose and outcome
Experience	Functionally focussed Specialists, experts	Specialists, experts Silo	Breadth and depth of experience rewarded
Behaviours	Promotes team Communication is key	Formal, traditional Protective	Opportunistic, fleet of foot Copes well with change
Networking	Cross-functional	Status driven	Spans functional and geographic boundaries
Recognition	Team achievements	Personal success and 'time served'	Team achievements and personal network

The 'network principle'

The 'network principle' has some common features:

- essential characteristics
- establishing the culture
- barriers to change
- unblocking organizations.

Essential characteristics

Networked organizations have advantages, not solely because of their internal characteristics, but also because of their ability to compete.

Essential characteristics of networked organizations are that they are:

- innovative
- flexible
- fast-footed.

Innovative

Innovation is the key to survival in the highly competitive environments in which organizations exist today. Truly innovative organizations encourage creativity at all levels.

In hierarchical organizations, ideas tend to be passed from one person to another rather like a baton in a relay race. If there is a weak link in the chain, the idea goes no further and creativity is quashed.

For people in an organization to innovate successfully, it is important that they are free to network between functions and geographies. This type of network is one in which ideas are challenges, encouraged and examined from many different vantage points. If ideas are good, they fan out, get picked up and adopted.

Innovation through networks:

- encourages
- refines
- reinforces
- recreates
- implements new ideas.

The culture and structure to support this innovation is characterized by open channels of communication that encourage and reward an enthusiastic exchange of ideas across functional and geographical boundaries.

Flexible

This style of organization demands new skills of managers and team members. Managers have to broaden their range of competences to become more effective as:

- team members
- catalysts
- communicators
- influencers/negotiators
- enablers
- informers
- project managers.

The traditional styles of management are not helpful in this new and evolving environment and managers, rather than working in a structured environment with a predictable pattern to their week, are much more likely to be faced with managing:

- cross-functional teams
- briefings
- brainstorming groups

- continuous improvement groups
- focus groups.

Managers who thrive in these environments are open to different views and approaches and are not threatened by change or by the unknown.

Fast-footed

Fast-footed organizations are those that are able to respond rapidly to changes in the demands placed upon them from:

- employees
- customers
- suppliers
- the (extended) community in which they exist
- the Political, Economic, Social and Technological environment (PEST).

There is no substitute for keeping your ear close to the ground, hearing and acting upon new ideas and developing trends.

Organizational structures have to be able to withstand the pressures of these new demands. If they are too brittle, or too inflexible, they will shatter. Flatter structures and networked organizations will assist in the process of toughening up and developing the kind of resilience that will enable them to respond to the complexities of the environment. However, the speed and complexity of organizations requires an effective network for managers to survive.

Establishing the culture

Regardless of the dominant style of your organization, there will be aspects of it that you will wish to retain and those that need revising. Unless there is a crisis in your industry or your organization, the adjustments that need to be made in order to become network-oriented need not be dramatic. Indeed, it may take some time to encourage people to change their behaviour. However, with constant reminders, reinforcement and reward, this can be accelerated.

When trying to establish a network culture, employees will need to know exactly what the organization is trying to achieve. Messages coming down from the top should be reinforced time and time again. Senior managers need to be seen to practise what they preach.

If you occupy a secure position in a traditionally hierarchical organization, networking may seem self-defeating. Sharing information may be perceived as giving power away. However, it is a two-way process and can, in the right conditions, enrich everyone.

But first, the conditions in which new behaviours can emerge must be put in place. These will only take root if everyone understands the change and can see its value. The following imperatives will help to fuel the change:

- Recognize individual and team contributions.
- Encourage career paths across functional boundaries.
- Remove functional focus from analysis.
- Instil discipline of broader perspective.
- Encourage cross-functional communication.
- Share organizational information.
- Support change with training and development.
- Monitor and evaluate all of these processes.

By doing this, you are, in essence, capitalizing on the expertise contained within the organization. This involves recognition and action. Try some simple steps such as building project teams across functional boundaries, introducing network mentors, identifying behavioural role models, offering coaching and support. Create opportunities that will naturally encourage networking: continuous improvement groups, quality forums, brainstorming activities, job shadowing and social functions.

Networked organizations are not constrained by the boundaries of the organizational structure. They look outside for examples of good practice, innovation and success. Look beyond your organizations at:

- competitors (benchmarking – as a minimum standard)
- customers
- suppliers
- professional bodies
- conferences
- research
- possibilities for joint projects or joint ventures.

In multinational organizations, additional mechanisms are required to facilitate communication across national borders. Such mechanisms include:

- email
- teleconferencing and Webex
- exchange visits
- international training and development
- newsletters
- international conferences
- intranet (and social networking).

Networking should be encouraged between opposite numbers in the organization and these opposite number networks should be tapped too. The exchange of experience in similar roles but dissimilar contexts is bound to be valuable and stimulate new ideas and approaches to the role.

Barriers to change

There are a number of different stumbling blocks that prevent effective and efficient networking. These come in the following forms:

- inertia
- fear
- ignorance.

Inertia

Inertia is often found in organizations that do not place a high importance on networking. These are likely to be the more traditional types of organizational structure that may believe that networking is idle gossip and has no value. These organizations often like to keep the channels of communication distinct and sealed.

Fear

Fear stems from the belief that control will be lost and that those who don't believe in networking will sabotage all efforts to change the culture. Control is an interesting issue. If too much of it is exerted, people identify subversive techniques to get around it. This results in a two-tier culture, the overt and the covert. This sits in direct opposition to the culture of a networked organization. Too little control, on the other hand, results in frustration and a loss of respect for those who occupy the positions where control is expected of them. A firm but receptive approach is generally the most effective.

Fear is exhibited in different ways. It may show itself in retrenchment where ideas, information and power are held possessively. It also may show itself in lack of co-operation and passive/aggressive behaviour. Organizations that contain those who do not want to share information for fear of losing their positional power may hear phrases like:

Mind your own business!
If you need the information, I'll give it to you!
Did you not know!?

Ignorance

Many people do not possess natural networking skills, so these must be developed and encouraged so that the new culture has a good chance of becoming established.

Often people think that the only component of networking is technology. This is merely a tool so we do not view it as a network in its own right. Networking is about human interactions. These interactions can be facilitated through communication technology but never replaced by it.

People in organizations hold a lot of experience and many skills that are not well advertised. Some of them are related to their professional roles, others are personal. It is amazing what talents you can unearth when you spend time networking.

Unblocking organizations

Variety is exciting, creative and dynamic and needs to be celebrated. Recognition of transferable skills and qualities need to be expressed in a way that will mobilize the workforce and motivate people to network and give more of their worth. If a match can be made between individual and organizational objectives, all the activities that take place within the workplace will contribute towards the overall strategic objectives of the organization.

The secret behind a successful shift to a networking culture can be remembered using the '4 Cs':

● Clear goal and commitment from the top
● Communication (four times over!)
● Constant and consistent reinforcement
● Celebration of success

There is hardly ever enough communication. This is pivotal!

Inter-organizational networks

Organizations can benefit greatly from careful strategic positioning in relation to other organizations' products and services. What attracts a customer to another product or service could equally well attract a customer to your own. For years, washing machine manufacturers have struck up beneficial relationships with detergent manufacturers. One carries the recommendation of the other – they go hand in hand – and together, they aim for the same target market with more force and precision than they could do alone.

These synergistic relationships now extend beyond the mere marrying of products and services to the physical positioning of retail outlets. With industrial parks and suburban shopping centres now firmly established in most economic cultures, many such relationships exist. McDonald's or Pizza Hut can often be found on the same sites as certain retail stores or entertainment venues. Customers are much more inclined to visit a shopping centre if many of their consumer objectives can be achieved in one fell swoop.

The same is true of more exclusive retailers. Haute-couture designer shops or exclusive department stores are co-located to bring in larger numbers of shoppers.

Summary

Organizations dominate our lives. It is perhaps more helpful to understand them as communities of people that need to interact rather than treat them as entities that are impermeable to human expression. In this way, we can create pathways to those people that can assist us in our career progression.

Finding supportive coaches or mentors is a good way to use the organizational network. Peers or senior managers are often happy to give back something to those people in the organization who will contribute to its success in the future. They will give you a listening ear, help you to understand the politics and rules of survival, introduce you to those who can offer you new opportunities and give you feedback before you take a wrong turn. It will be your turn to do this for others in the future but for the time being, see yourself as a worthy human asset that will pay dividends in the end.

By understanding the structure and style of your own organization in this way, and by building robust channels of communication, you will put yourself in the driving seat of your own professional life.

SUNDAY
MONDAY
TUESDAY
WEDNESDAY
THURSDAY
FRIDAY
SATURDAY

Questions

Answer the following questions honestly, reflecting on the network nature of your organization:

1. **How would you describe your organizational structure?**
   a) Flat ☐
   b) Hierarchical ☐
   c) Networked ☐
   d) None of these ☐

2. **What networking do you see in your organization?**
   a) Informal gatherings ☐
   b) Communication/social events taking place ☐
   c) Communication with colleagues ☐
   d) People doing their work, heads down and isolated ☐

3. **Where are the hubs in your organization?**
   a) Senior executives ☐
   b) Line managers ☐
   c) Those whose work crosses functional boundaries ☐
   d) Everyone ☐

4. **What are the most common barriers to networking in your organization?**
   a) There are none ☐
   b) Inertia ☐
   c) Fear ☐
   d) Ignorance ☐

5. **What are the most common forms of communication in your organization?**
   a) Email ☐
   b) Telephone ☐
   c) Meetings ☐
   d) Communication is not encouraged ☐

6. **What exists to cultivate networking in your organization?**
   a) Training and development ☐
   b) Company gatherings ☐
   c) None ☐
   d) Social events ☐

7. **What inter-organizational initiatives exist in your organization?**
   a) Best practice exchanges ☐
   b) Secondments/job sharing ☐
   c) Joint ventures/strategic alliances ☐
   d) None ☐

8. **How often do you network beyond your immediate working environment?**
   a) Daily–weekly ☐
   b) Monthly–yearly ☐
   c) Less than every two years ☐
   d) Never ☐

9. **Which of the '4 Cs' operate in your organization?**
   a) Clear goal and commitment from the top ☐
   b) Communication ☐
   c) Constant reinforcement ☐
   d) Celebration of success ☐

10. **What is the culture of your organization?**
    a) Innovative ☐
    b) Flexible ☐
    c) Fast-footed ☐
    d) Fragmented ☐

WEDNESDAY

Professional networks

Professional networks assist you in your career progression. They can provide information, support, influence and development. Above all, they are a vehicle through which you can identify and create opportunities.

Career progression

- Information
  - What is the best strategy?
  - Who is the expert?
- Support
  - How do you see it?
  - How would you feel?
- Influence
  - Who should I be talking to?
  - Can you introduce me?
- Development
  - How can I get up to speed?
  - What do I need to be aware of?
  - How can I find out what I don't know?

Professional networks are built around common work interests and tasks. Your organizational network is likely to be a subset of your professional network. However, professional networks can consume other networks to which you affiliate such as clubs, professional societies, alumni and trade associations.

Professional networks have no geographical bounds: they extend right around the globe – particularly if they are virtual.

As a professional, you have automatic licence to tap into the network in the course of carrying out your professional duties or on the wing of a business proposition or idea. Indeed, it is an approach such as this that will lead to the creation of profitable alliances and the building of business opportunities. In this chapter, we will cover the following areas of professional networks:

● What are they?
● It's a small world
● Building bridges
● Feed and water regularly

What are they?

For simplicity, we have divided professional networks into different categories: intra- and extra-organizational, professional organizations and virtual networks. The various forms of professional networks have different codes of conduct so it is useful to consider these and try to determine what they may be.

Intra-organizational

These networks consist of:

● colleagues
● peers

- superiors
- bosses
- casual informants (who form the grapevine)
- politically motivated people (those with career aspirations or change agents)
- personal alliances (friends and informal social acquaintances).

The code of conduct for making connections in the working environment is fairly well defined from a professional standpoint. Understanding the undercurrents that create the political flavour, however, is the key to your success in working in an organizational network effectively. These invisible ebbs and flows need to be considered from a safe distance before entering the fray.

Bide your time. Only when you feel sure that you have correctly identified the various allegiances that exist in the organization is it time for you to form your own alliances. Don't rush in where angels fear to tread. Others' perceptions of you will be coloured by those you fraternize with.

Although you are more or less bound to fall into a political minefield at some stage, persevere – you will soon learn to trust your observations and, with your successes, develop faith in your instincts.

Extra-organizational

Extra-organizational networks consist of:

- competitors
- customers
- suppliers
- agencies
- joint venture partners
- strategic alliances
- family and friends
- former colleagues
- college/university networks
- alumni groups.

When engaging with those outside your working environment, you will need to be aware that all your communications and actions will go towards creating an impression of you and your organization. Your personal integrity will be on show so it is important that you manage the perception of others in what is a small world. You will often find that people you connect with outside your organization have a feeder back into it, albeit through a different channel.

People have a need to judge and they will use whatever material is available to them to base their judgements upon. If you make a wrong move in the initial stages of your relationship with someone, usually within the first few seconds of meeting them, it will determine the dominant impression that they have of you. Recreating or altering an impression is disproportionately harder than creating one in the first place!

Professional network organizations

Professional network organizations include:

- Professional websites (for example LinkedIn®)
- Professional groups, associations and clubs (for example Chambers of Commerce, Writers' Guild, Women's Business Network)
- Professional bodies (for example Chartered Management Institute)

Many network organizations now exist. They are designed to facilitate networking among those with similar interests, values and professions. Some of these organizations are welcoming of new members; others are closed.

The vehicles of communication for activating a network are things such as: regular meetings, seminars, workshops, group activities, social events, blogs, webinars and so forth. Although not everyone's cup of tea, they are extremely useful ways of contacting a target group of others who are highly likely to want to connect with you – professionally or personally.

Professional websites

Virtual networks, held on the Internet, have become extremely popular and much value can be gained from them. These hold the technological answer to the rapid and efficient exchange of contacts and information. Indeed, they have become so ubiquitous that a lack of presence on a website, such as

LinkedIn®, can disadvantage you by leaving you out of the way of serendipitous contacts – either from those you have known in the past or from potential future colleagues.

Dependency on a virtual network, however, can have its limitations. It cannot replace the face-to-face benefits of building a relationship or tackling mutual business interests. It also prevents the interpretation of non-verbal signals, which form the largest proportion of the messages we convey in our communication.

Being on a professional website allows you to present your credentials to a wide, but select, audience. Accompanied by a photograph and way of communicating your activities and new connections, there is an element of dynamism that compensates for the more traditional, face-to-face, professional network. However, there is nothing to replace the alchemy of a personal meeting and often, meaningful virtual connections result in this.

Professional groups, associations and clubs
There are many professional groups and associations that will be known to you through your specialization (profession), aspiration (cause) or attribute (gender) that you share uniquely with others. These can be fruitful environments for support, information, practical assistance, advice and the comfort of sharing a common language and common problems.

Often, professional groups and associations host networking events to bring members together regularly. Although membership can be used as a shortcut to convey credibility, it also provides more practical support in progressing your career.

Professional bodies

A professional body upholds the standards of your work, through a Charter, which has been awarded by an academic institution, legislative or sovereign power. Coaching associations or management institutes are examples of this kind of professional body. Members must adhere to the standards of practice, and honour the code of conduct, that is set out in the Charter – or their membership may be at risk.

These professional bodies make a statement about the level of your professionalism and often obviate the need for proof through other, lengthier, means. Membership of some organizations and even to a particular standard, level or grade may be a condition of employment.

It's a small world

A good professional network can support you in your:

- role
- career
- personal life.

Your role

Everyone requires the means for professional enhancement to stay relevant, ahead and successful. Networks can provide you with this in a variety of ways:

- feedback
- know-how
- benchmarking
- management information
- problem-solving
- development.

Your professional network can act as your safety net, providing opportunities to share best practice, thoughts and opinions in a confidential environment that is not constrained by the boundaries of your organization.

Professional networks ensure that you keep up to date and informed of the latest developments in your arena. They provide a mechanism through which you can access knowledge and exchange advice, ideas and insights of professional significance. They also provide an environment in which you can learn from others who have already encountered situations that are new to you.

Some form of self and role evaluation is essential for all professionals. Professional networks provide the professional standards, levels of competence and goals against which you can judge yourself and through which you can identify your development needs. Every professional should take responsibility for their own continuous professional development (CPD) and professional networks give you access to people who enable you to benchmark yourself.

Your career

Your professional responsibility extends beyond the need for CPD in your role, to responsibility for your career.

Career benefits include:

- feedback
- assistance
- exposure
- early warning system.

Professional networks are unique in that they can provide the means of receiving open and objective feedback. Although not always comfortable, you can develop an understanding of how you are perceived by others who know your career path. Not only can they give you candid and valuable feedback, but also visibility and exposure to new people and opportunities. On Thursday, we will give you more insights into networking for career development.

Your personal life

Professional networks can support you in a variety of other ways. Personal benefits can include:

- new social circles
- recommendations
- referrals.

Social circles are often created as a result of networking in the professional arena. These will transcend the professional networks from which they came. If this happens, it is a bonus. However, be alert to the confusion that can arise around the liberties friends can take as compared to those professional colleagues can take. It would be hard for your boss – and perhaps for you – if you asked for a babysitting favour, for example!

Building bridges

Networks can emerge and disappear like a mirage. They can be created in order to meet a specific goal and dissolved once this goal has been met.

When a temporary network is required, it needs to be mapped, monitored and evaluated carefully. After its dissolution, some of the good contacts that you have made may be preserved and positioned in another of your networks.

In order to make the most of the potential a network holds, it is important to be clear about what you want from it.

What do you want from your network?

● A new position?
● News of job opportunities?
● Entry to an 'inner circle'?

By identifying what you want from your network, you will be clear about selecting its members.

Feed and water regularly

A network is only as good as the care and attention you give it. This is not necessarily an arduous activity – it can become almost instinctive over time. Nevertheless, your networks will need general maintenance on a regular basis.

Maintain your network by:

● pruning
● growing
● investing
● rewarding.

Pruning

It is likely that you have relationships in your network that no longer serve or benefit you. These relationships can sap your energy and divert your focus unless they are pruned and discarded.

Growing

Consciously and consistently add to your network. Be very clear of your goals and be sure of the key players and their potential to assist you. It is very easy to waste the potential of a good contact.

Investing

Keeping a network alive and active requires an investment of time and energy. Take care to be sensitive and courteous. It would be a shame to milk the network too much and lose your credibility and the goodwill others have for you. Think about what you can do for others and make the effort to pro-act.

Rewarding

Don't forget to thank those who have assisted you. Showing appreciation is as important as maintenance. Is there anything tangible you can do to exchange the favour you have received?

Summary

Professional networks can be powerful mechanisms if you are clear about:

● what you want from them
● how to make them work for your benefit.

To demonstrate the breadth and potential of your professional network, try the following:

1 Select a high profile name – such as Barack Obama, Oprah Winfrey or Richard Branson – and try to identify how many 'handshakes' you would need to contact that person. (We would be surprised if you were more than four or five handshakes away from these people!)

2 You may already have some superb contacts in your network but try thinking about your network from a different vantage point and see whether you can identify where these contacts could lead you.

3 In relation to your future career aspirations, ask yourself who would be the most valuable people you could connect with. Map out the route to meeting these people and initiate some meetings.

SUNDAY

MONDAY

TUESDAY

WEDNESDAY

THURSDAY

FRIDAY

SATURDAY

Professional networks checklist:

- Identify your networks
  - Intra-organizational
  - Extra-organizational
  - Professional

- Clarify your goals
- Build relationships
- Monitor, manage and review your network
- Networking is never one-way. To support the existence of your professional networks you need to play your part in serving them.

Questions

Answer the following questions honestly, reflecting on your professional network.

1. **How do you use your professional network?**
   a) For information ☐
   b) For support ☐
   c) For influence ☐
   d) For feedback and development ☐

2. **To which professional network organizations do you belong?**
   a) Professional websites ☐
   b) Professional associations ☐
   c) Professional bodies ☐
   d) None of the above ☐

3. **How do you maintain your professional network?**
   a) Prune ☐
   b) Grow ☐
   c) Invest ☐
   d) I don't. It takes care of itself ☐

4. **How has your professional network assisted you?**
   a) New job ☐
   b) Introductions ☐
   c) Business opportunities ☐
   d) It hasn't ☐

5. **How have you helped those in your professional network?**
   a) Bringing people together ☐
   b) As a carrier of information ☐
   c) Sending articles, papers, conference details ☐
   d) I don't engage with my professional network ☐

6. **Looking over the map of your professional network:**
   a) Who's missing? ☐
   b) Who's no longer actively assisting you? ☐
   c) What professional network? ☐
   d) Is there anyone who can link you to another network? ☐

7. **How much time do you spend managing your professional network?**
   a) I give it daily attention ☐
   b) I think about my network when I have a need ☐
   c) I only notice it when someone wants something from me ☐
   d) I rarely give my attention to my network ☐

8. **How many professional websites are you active on?**
   a) I am active on more than 3 ☐
   b) I am active on 2–3 ☐
   c) I am active on 1–2 ☐
   d) I am not on a professional website ☐

9. **How often do you update your profile?**

a) I review it weekly ☐
b) When I receive notifications about my contacts ☐
c) I am active on my site when I have a specific need ☐
d) My original profile remains unaltered ☐

10. **How do you feel about professional networking?**

a) I enjoy meeting people of like mind ☐
b) I find it useful when I need to achieve something ☐
c) It feels 'manipulative' to me so I network rarely ☐
d) I am never proactive ☐

THURSDAY

Networking for career development

The concept of networking has its origins in the context of careers. Most people at some stage in their career will have used their network to aid their advancement. Your first job, Saturday job, or summer jobs may have come about because of a contact your parents, family or friends had. When older, you develop a more sophisticated version of this as your network extends beyond your personal networks.

Think about your career:

How did you hear about the jobs?

How did the recruiter hear about you?

This traditional and well-tested means of developing and advancing your career is even more important now that organizations are flatter, allowing fewer opportunities for upward promotion. In these new organizations, the way people group together is far more fluid. This has consequences for the traditional management career and the expectations that many managers hold about their futures.

65

Traditionally, managers had certain expectations about their careers, which were based on the pyramid structure of organizations. When you entered an organization, your career was pretty much mapped out and you could be clear about your end point, the route between now and then, and the timescales involved.

These days, successful careers are based on networking, not on a traditional career path carved in stone. Knowing how to network to advance your career is an essential survival skill. To survive means using your career networks responsibly and ethically.

You should take responsibility for your career and invest time, energy and money to ensure that your career goal in the short, medium and long term is achievable. This responsibility is as important if you intend to stay with one organization as it is if you intend to move. To place the responsibility for your career onto any organization is to neglect it.

You need to think about your career and how to develop your network to benefit you professionally.

In this chapter we will cover the following:

● Begin with the end in mind!
● It's who you know
● What to say after you've said 'Hello'

Begin with the end in mind!

If we were to pose a simple question to you such as 'Who are you?', we would not be surprised if you hesitated and began by answering 'I'm an operations manager' or 'I'm a training manager'. We tend to think of ourselves as what we do rather than who we are. This can have its dangers. In the past, as a result of the changing needs of the organizations in which we worked, we probably became what was demanded of us with little thought or reflection about what we enjoyed or what we did best.

A successful career is made up of many components: job types, styles and content, development, fulfilment and fit.

Getting this right depends on understanding yourself. What are your:

- skills?
- strengths?
- limitations?
- values?
- interests?
- pleasures?
- achievements?

Do not focus only on your education, skills and experience to formulate your next move. Focus on what makes you unique and how you could contribute to an organization. Also, focus on what you enjoy. Natural enthusiasm is easily conveyed and extremely contagious – and opportunities are in short supply. Communicating your value with enthusiasm is important if you are to outshine the competition and distinguish yourself as the best candidate for the job.

Where do you want to go?

Having taken an honest and thorough look at yourself, how clear are you about where you want to go – your destination? While your future may seem hazy, some idea of where you're going helps you to plan your moves and to gauge your progress.

Where you want to go can have many stages: perhaps the simplest way to think of these stages is as your short, medium and long-term goals.

Some people have goals that are not work related but do have an impact their work. One manager we met had the goal of retiring at 50 so that he could concentrate on his interests. This affected his career and his career choices directly because he needed to achieve a level of income to support him in his ambition. Others have goals such as embarking on a second career. In this case, they will need to invest in the appropriate networks to ensure that this is realized.

In the short to medium term, your goals may be related to more tangible things such as:

- location
- function
- field
- rewards
- work style
- colleagues
- organization.

Goals need reviewing regularly as they might be unrealistic and under- or over-ambitious. The rapidly changing business environment and the high level of uncertainty can significantly affect our goals, and over time goals can change as we develop.

Your end point

Your end point, aspiration or goal can then be built into your daily life so that you can manage yourself each day to be and to do what really matters to you most. Every decision you make will be in the context of your goal so by definition, you will be moving towards it steadily and certainly. This helps you to target your network. Your targets could be triggered by:

- contacts in your preferred locality
- role models
- functional experts
- network 'hubs' in your specialist field.

It's who you know

Your current contacts are the raw material for your career development. They, in turn, have contacts of their own. What you have at your disposal now is an enormous network – and made even larger (and more accessible) if you add yourself to a professional networking website.

Who do you know?

As a start, organize this raw material into a database of contacts – or examine your contacts on your professional website. Think about the following information for each person:

● title/position
● organization
● contact details
● address/location
● how you know this person
● when you met this person
● what kind of relationship do you enjoy with this person
● who else they are connected to in your network
● what networks they are able to access on your behalf.

Keep note of your contact with each person in your network. Include:

● the date of your contact
● a brief outline of the conversation or meeting you had
● any memorable information to refer back to
● the outcome of your meeting
● the date of any follow-up.

Even if you love your job and have no intention of moving at the moment, it would be good to start managing your network now. The perfect time to organize and develop your network is when you don't need it!

The networking process is gradual and requires investment. Building relationships with professional or personal contacts that have the potential to move you towards your long-term career goal is never wasted. The first step in targeted networking of this nature is to identify 'black holes' in your network. Are there gaps in your network between your current job and your desired job?

Maybe you already have contacts in the department, division, organization or industry that you wish to be part of. If not, see whether you can find a point of entry.

Your aim, in doing this, is to establish a network that is made up of contacts that serve you in one of the following ways.

Your contact:

- sees a job advertisement and draws your attention to it
- receives information about a local organization and passes it to you
- knows a recruiter who specializes in your function and introduces you to him or her
- knows someone with influence or information and orchestrates a meeting
- identifies a vacancy in his or her organizations and informs you of it
- offers you a position in his or her organization.

A quality contact could be someone in a position to offer you a job or arrange an interview. However, anyone who has a pair of relevant ears or eyes is a valuable contact.

You cannot always be in the right place at the right time but by developing your network, you have more of a chance of hearing about, seeing or recognizing the right opportunities.

With your goal in mind, it is important to think about who can offer you help. It is often the people you have the weakest links with – your old contacts that have been dormant for years and have almost been forgotten – who can be the most effective in your career progression. Weak links can provide you with new information and essential bridges to other groups and networks. Your strongest links will tend to be functioning well already so they will only need reminding of your aspirations and needs.

Who can you get to know?

You may also need to extend your network and you can do this through using:

- professional websites
- college alumni
- conferences
- committees and project teams
- professional or trade associations
- sponsors who will introduce you to other networks.

Career visibility

Mobility is the key to network building because it can lead to visibility. Make and take every opportunity to move into new networks. Explore new:

- places
- people
- opportunities.

Volunteer to take temporary assignments with another group, division or subsidiary. Join new committees and teams, especially those with representatives from other departments in your organization. Attend and participate in business and social events.

Build networks through:

- outside meetings
- conferences
- seminars
- professional events
- exhibitions.

Remember, the point of this visibility exercise is to meet different people who bridge different business and social circles. You may also want to try local events such as a village or town meeting, parent-teacher association, lectures or any other event where you can naturally meet other people from diverse backgrounds. It is amazing how often you come across someone who is connected to your world in one way or another.

Suggested activity:

For the rest of the week, make notes of all the people you meet during the course of each day. Indicate the networking potential of each contact and identify the point of convergence in your respective lives.

What to say after you've said 'Hello'

Be aware of the people you need in your network. Always remember this and plan your networks thoughtfully. You need to ask yourself repeatedly, 'How can I meet the people I need to?'

It is one thing meeting these people, but quite another being able to benefit from the meeting. This is often the point at which many people fall; they have extensive networks but are not skilled at using them.

Think carefully about how you build productive relationships and how to establish rapport.

Building blocks
- Mentor's recommendation
- Your reputation or that of the organization
- Your accomplishments
- Position in the community
- Mutuality
  - An issue you share
  - An organization you both belong to
  - Work or life experience
  - Interests

Prove you are worth talking to: prepare a short summary of your career. Make it positive and base it on recent and relevant achievements. Be succinct and deliver it with energy and enthusiasm. Also, state your career goal.

How can they help?

It is important to communicate how they can help. Their support could be invaluable and information is always useful.

Information
Is the business expanding or shrinking?
What organizations are doing well?
What developments are current or planned?
Who are the key people who make recruitment decisions?
What opportunities are available?
What are the salary levels?

Support

Seek comments on your résumé.

Get advice on your approach.

Ask for some doors to be opened for you.

Get advice/feedback on an interview presentation.

Some people will simply be too busy to spend time with you. But they may know others who can help. Always end with the question: *Who else should I be talking to?*

This is the point at which you are building the bridges between different circles or networks.

If you are asking for an introduction, be aware of what the other person thinks of you. If he or she has any doubts about your abilities, you may be better to talk to someone else.

Script and rehearse what you intend to say. Practice makes perfect. You don't get a second chance to make a first impression!

If someone has taken the time to meet with you and given you valuable information, keep him or her up to date. If you have followed their lead, tell them of your progress. If they haven't heard from you for some time, they may assume that you have been successful in your quest but they may also be slightly fed up that you haven't 'closed the loop' with some feedback and a 'thank you'.

Summary

On first appearance, success may appear to have come easily to some. While they may, indeed, be blessed with advantage, they are much more likely to have developed their skills over many years and built a valuable network that delivers a return on their investment.

To use your network to develop your career, you need to have a good understanding of your skills, competences and strengths. Once you understand yourself to this extent, you can focus on where you want to get to and begin with an end in mind. This will enable you to articulate your career goals clearly to those who are best placed to help you.

The value of networking is that you are constantly advertising yourself. You are shaping the future by:

- being in the right place at the right time
- knowing the right people
- presenting yourself credibly
- sending the right messages.

Of course, this is not a one-way street. Those who are able to help you will only do so if they feel that you reciprocate in kind.

SUNDAY
MONDAY
TUESDAY
WEDNESDAY
THURSDAY
FRIDAY
SATURDAY

Networking for career development checklist:

- Know yourself and your aspirations
- Communicate your career goals
- Nurture your contacts
- Follow up with feedback and a 'thank you'.

Questions

Answer the following questions honestly, reflecting on your network for career development.

1. **How do you describe your short-, medium- and long-term career goals?**
   a) I am very clear about what I want to achieve ☐
   b) I know what I want to do next ☐
   c) I like to remain open to opportunities ☐
   d) I have no idea what I want to do in my career ☐

2. **How do you manage your network for career advancement?**
   a) I am present – but relatively inactive – on a professional website ☐
   b) I am present – and active – on a professional website ☐
   c) I make sure that I network regularly ☐
   d) I don't manage my network at all ☐

3. **When building your professional website, what do you feel is important?**
   a) That my information is up to date ☐
   b) I make connections with those identified by the system to be relevant ☐
   c) I put my photo and my CV on the site and accept invitations to join other networks ☐
   d) The fact that I'm there is enough ☐

4. **How have you benefitted, career-wise, from your network in the past?**
   a) I have been sent helpful information ☐
   b) I have had doors opened for me ☐
   c) I have been offered at least one job ☐
   d) My network ☐

5. **Where could you build your network for career advancement?**
   a) College and university alumni ☐
   b) Former colleagues ☐
   c) Professional associations ☐
   d) By attending conferences ☐

6. **How do you respond when someone asks you for career help?**
   a) I take time to listen to their needs and give advice ☐
   b) I think about who's in my network and contact them ☐
   c) I arrange and host a meeting if there is mutual interest ☐
   d) I'm too busy managing my own career to assist with anyone else's! ☐

7. **What extracurricular activities are you involved in?**
   a) I am a volunteer ☐
   b) I sit on a local committee ☐
   c) I socialize with people in my community ☐
   d) I don't have any extracurricular activities ☐

8. **How prepared are you to ask for career help?**
a) I contact members of my network readily ☐
b) I think about what I can do to encourage others' assistance ☐
c) I find it hard to ask for help but do ☐
d) I tend not to ask for career help ☐

9. **How do you build your reputation and visibility?**
a) I am an active networker ☐
b) I write articles ☐
c) I give presentations at conferences ☐
d) I like to be invisible! ☐

10. **How do you keep up to date with what's going on in your professional world?**
a) I have a mentor who makes sure that I am plugged in ☐
b) I read the business sections of the newspaper ☐
c) I attend events and seminars ☐
d) I rely on what is circulated around the organization ☐

FRIDAY

Social
networking

So far, we have looked at networks from different vantage points: personal, organizational, professional and those that facilitate career advancement. Social networking is something else again. A phenomenon that has swept the world along with the advent of the Internet, social networks have become the face, eyes and ears of individuals on the world – for good and for bad!

Social networking sites are proliferating in many different arenas, spanning both professional and personal settings and they support a diverse range of interests and orientations. They allow people to create or join web-based communities that resonate with them for one reason or another – which may be for career advancement or just for fun. It is a way of reaching out, making contact, disclosing personal information, accessing new information, sharing experiences, building relationships, finding opportunities and offering support.

In this chapter, we're going to look at several aspects of social networking. However, we are not going to do a review of all social networking sites, nor are we going to guide you through building your own site. Rather, we will be raising general issues and using them to think about this phenomenon.

Today we will focus on:

- What's new about networking on a social networking site?
- What does joining a social network entail?
- Is social networking addictive?
- What level of privacy can you expect?
- What are the pros and cons of social networking?
- What are the dos and don'ts of social networking?
- Using social networks in work time
- Social networking vs professional websites
- What is Twitter®?
- What does Twitter® do for businesses?

What's new about networking on a social networking site?

Although sites enable new acquaintances to be made, by far the most common connection is made with people who are already in your near and 'once removed' network. They may be people whom you have known in the past or people known to those with whom you are already in close contact, either physically or virtually. Social networking sites are successful in making these extended networks tangible and allowing you to build relationships that you might not otherwise have built.

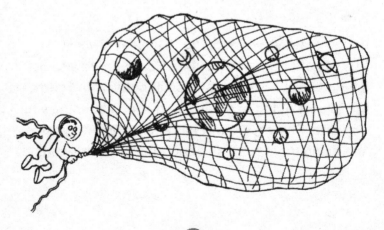

In addition, social networking allows you to reach out to those you probably would never have met in the normal course of your life. Profiles of individuals held on such sites contain all the information others need to decide whether to enter into a correspondence. In this way, new relationships begin their life. Sometimes these are fleeting. Sometimes they are robust and lead to long-term friendships. Sometimes they lead to love and marriage. And, sadly, sometimes they are exploitive.

What does joining a social network entail?

To join a social networking site, you will usually be asked to disclose some personal information about yourself. This may include:

- a photograph – you have an option to omit the photograph but on a professional network such as LinkedIn®, it may be a good idea to include one. On a social networking site, such as Facebook®, Myspace® or Bebo®, people are often tempted to submit an image that is a caricature or symbol that they feel conveys something about them, whether it be humorous, idiosyncratic or oblique!
- work and educational achievements
- personal/professional aims and aspirations
- email address and website links.

And on a more personally orientated social networking site

- your gender
- your birthday
- your relationship status
- interests, hobbies, group membership and causes being pursued
- photographs/videos.

On most sites, you can select which bits of this information enter the public domain and can set levels of access that screen out those people you'd rather not be in contact with. You will be asked to make connections with those you know to build your network of 'friends'. ('Friend' is a term used whether or not you know the person you're in contact with.) Once this has been done, you will be offered the names of those you may know through your emerging network. These are the 'friends' of those you know. These close acquaintances will form the hub of your network.

Activity on the site can take many different forms. You can share photographs, videos, links to other sites, messages, jokes, games... all these create the kaleidoscopic joy of a social networking site!

On professional networking sites, the material you share is work orientated and the purpose of sharing it is to build your reputation or further your career. Instead of 'friends', your network will be comprised of 'connections'.

If you are building a professional network, make sure you have a clear purpose and understand the route by which your invitations have arrived. If you wish to accept an invitation from someone you think will be able to assist you in some way, consider what you can do for them that will incentivize them to do so. This will enable you to start building a reciprocal relationship that will enable you to reach your career goals.

On one professional networking site, this note pops up on joining: 'Welcome to ... – The world's largest business referral network'. As an added bonus, if 20 of your colleagues accept your invite, you'll unlock the 'social networker' badge and be showcased throughout the entire site, putting you in front of thousands of potential clients and referral sources.

Some sites rely upon 'old' acquaintances or shared educational experiences to form a network. 'Ever wondered what happened to so-and-so?' they ask. Or 'Find old school friends', they promise. It is amazing how people from the past become accessible through such sites, even those you'd all but forgotten.

Is social networking addictive?

In 2005, research suggested that young people were spending, on average, at least 1 hour 22 minutes on a variety of sites every day. As an average, this suggests that some people will be spending many more hours than this on their site. Indeed, it is thought possible to become addicted to social networking sites and there have been cases where people neglect their 'real' lives in order to live their 'virtual' lives.

Technology also allows you to access sites on the move, sites and alerts can be put on mobile phones as applications so that you're never more than a click away from your network and able to interact with your 'friends' in real time. You can also leave messages for those who are not logged on and enjoy the advantages of asynchronous communication.

What level of privacy can you expect?

At a time when digital communication can sweep the world in seconds, the question of whether or not there is any privacy is a good one.

It has been found that some young people, who spend a great deal of time on social networking sites, are willing to give personal information quite freely, with a false sense of security about its destination and use. Parents may set rules to control how their children use sites, such as how much time they can spend on a site or the level of parental involvement in selecting 'friends'.

However, it is possible, through various sites, to convey a message, whether it is benign or malign, to hundreds and thousands of people at one time. In several clicks, parties can be planned, flash mobs can be organized – where many people come together to perform in the street and riots can be incited.

Those who post messages on sites have no ultimate control over who reads and circulates the message. Messages can be hijacked and spread beyond the wishes of the messenger to find their way into groups or communities that the messenger would not intend. Once on the Internet, there is no way of retrieving and discarding the message. It is always there, somewhere. Recently, one young person, wishing to celebrate her exam success, announced a party at her parent's house and gave the address. Thousands of people turned up and the police had to be called to break up the party. Needless to say the house was trashed.

It is only recently, too, that Facebook®, Twitter® and BBM® (BlackBerry Messenger) have been used to bring people together to riot in the streets of major cities in the United Kingdom. The ease with which messages can be passed to large groups of people means that it is not only private networks but also extended networks that can be mobilized. This can happen in seconds to bring people together, to organize events or, in this case, a series of riots. Interestingly, the same approach was used to mobilize the cleaning up operation. 'What's sauce for the goose, is sauce for the gander!' Even more recently, two of the rioters who used Facebook® to incite people to destroy their local towns have received extensive prison terms.

There is no country or technology barrier that cannot be crossed using digital communication and there is virtually no control over the content or purpose of the messages. This casts new light on the notion of a 'free press', the consequences of which were inconceivable when it was first mooted in the 17th century.

What are the pros and cons of social networking?

On the one hand, sites allow you to make connections with others from around the world who you would otherwise not encounter. This creates a rare opportunity to build culturally diverse relationships and learn about others' work, lives and cultures.

On the other hand, you have limited control over the information others receive, and you cannot validate (with certainty) the invitations you receive to become 'friends' in their network. Sometimes people pose as 'friends' in order to gain access to your network. If you aren't aware of these 'scams', you could be vulnerable to their effects.

Particularly in the case of young people, anxious parents and bystanders should encourage prudence when inviting or accepting friendships and care in developing information and messages before making these public.

What are the dos and don'ts of social networking?

Do: Think about what would be the 'worst possible outcome' of putting your information on the web. This will help you censor and protect yourself.

Do: Think about what you wish to get from your social networking and choose your 'friends' and connections carefully – you can add, block or dismiss people if you wish.

Do: Set your levels of privacy so that your site can't be accessed freely.

Do: Manage the time you spend on sites. It is easy to get lost in a virtual world and forget your other priorities!

Do: Think twice about your invitations. If you haven't stayed in touch over the years, why do you think you'll want to be in touch now?

Don't: Enter a stream of consciousness that may get you into difficulty later. You may think your message is innocent or funny but others may not think so!

Don't: Put up contentious photographs of yourself. They could be viewed by those you wouldn't wish to see them, such as parents or potential employers.

Don't: Accept all the invitations you receive. Validate the integrity of the person who is inviting you to become a friend and block those that you know to be untrustworthy or unpleasant.

Don't: Assume your intentions will protect you! To ensure that you don't find yourself on the world stage with a damning message, try thinking about what would be the worst destination for your message and the consequences of it arriving there. By thinking twice, you may decide not to send it or write it in such a way that it won't do any damage – to either the sender or the recipient!

Using social networks in work time

Social networking has become so prolific that some organizations have banned the use of it in the working environment. It is too tempting, they feel, for people to spend their working hours socialising with their 'friends' and not engaging in productive activities. These are some of the reasons:

- They fear confidential material leaking through the social networks.
- Social networking can take up a large proportion of the corporate bandwidth.
- Research finds that huge financial losses occur as productivity dips in favour of social networking.
- There is a threat of web-borne viruses contaminating the organization's IT system.
- People are less likely to be available to their colleagues.

Yet other organizations encourage social networking, for the following reasons:

- It provides a 'snowballing' opportunity for marketing products and services – and brand.

- It provides a possible means of conducting market research.
- Social networking can be a modern means of facilitating the free exchange of information (and gossip) that takes place in all organizations anyway.
- It is a valuable conduit for disseminating organizational information and reinforcing the culture.

Some organizations may strike a balance. This may include:

- restricting access to certain social networking sites
- developing employees' awareness of the benefits and problems
- setting security levels
- creating policies to control what it is allowable to say and how to use the site
- establishing a corporate social networking site.

Social networking vs professional websites

Professional networking is a sub-set of the social networking phenomenon. Professional networking sites share the same technological platform as social networking sites, upon which you can build your professional network. In the same way, they help you do this by making connections with people in your professional field – and beyond. These may be former/current colleagues, bosses, prospective or actual clients, suppliers, friends in the same role or industry... and they help you access extended networks through your list of contacts.

Professional networks are more targeted than social networks and the 'terms of engagement' are more formal. For this reason, it is easier to stay in control of personal information, although there are no real safeguards to circulating information on the Internet.

Every time you are active on your site, your contacts will be notified of this. This underlines the importance of managing your site attentively so that you can be sure that your information is always up to date and relevant to your purposes.

What is Twitter®?

Twitter® is a way of sharing succinct pieces of information with millions of people. Using Twitter®, businesses are able to discover new information and share it widely.

The messages that are shared are restricted to 140 characters so that they are short and sweet – or not so sweet! The messages are public and anyone can read them. This 'rapid fire', 'sound bite' way of communicating has captured the imagination of many people, from celebrities to politicians to 'normal' folk. The audience for receiving specific 'tweets' can be thousands strong; you elect to follow tweets from certain people who interest you and the messages are sent in 'real time'.

What does Twitter® do for businesses?

Businesses use Twitter® to share information rapidly, to gather opinions and insights from the market and to build relationships with people who are interested in their business activities.

Because 'tweets' are restricted in size, they tend to be used for 'chatter' and keeping people connected. However, they can also be used for sending out announcements and key bits of information.

Summary

Never before has 'real time' communication been so available to such a vast number of people. This comes with the advantages and disadvantages of open access and unrestricted content.

The advantages of social networking bring visibility, an easy exchange of information, an instant channel for communication and access to people and events that might otherwise be off your radar. We could list the disadvantages in exactly the same way, but the quality and impression of the messages you send will determine people's perception of you, not only those in your close circle but those who hold the key to your future success as an employee or member of other networks that you might value.

Young people have known nothing different. The gateway to the globe is open by way of information and virtual connections.

Social networking, still in its infancy, needs to be used thoughtfully with attention being given to its management and control. Don't forget, it's not just about how YOU use social networking sites; it's about how OTHERS use them too.

With many routes in, you cannot guarantee that your confidences will be kept. They can just as easily be propelled around the globe.

Professional websites have emerged alongside social networking sites. Using the same underlying technology, these sites allow people to build their professional networks and advance their careers, but the same rules and considerations apply.

Questions

Answer the following questions honestly, reflecting on your social and professional networks.

1. How many social networking sites are you present on?
a) 4–5 (or more) ❏
b) 3–4 ❏
c) 1–3 ❏
d) None ❏

2. How often do you access your social network?
a) Multiple times every day ❏
b) Once every day ❏
c) Every week/month ❏
d) Hardly ever ❏

3. What do you use your social networking site for?
a) To build contacts ❏
b) To communicate with an extended network ❏
c) Solely for social purposes ❏
d) To find work ❏

4. Where are you when you access your site?
a) Anywhere – mobile ❏
b) With friends ❏
c) Home ❏
d) Work ❏

5. How many contacts do you have on your social networking sites?
a) 1–20 ❏
b) 21–100 ❏
c) 101–500 ❏
d) More than 500 ❏

6. What is the nature of your contacts?
a) A mix of personal and professional contacts ❏
b) Colleagues and professional acquaintances ❏
c) An extended network of family and friends ❏
d) Personal friends and family ❏

7. What is the main purpose of your social network?
a) To collect as many 'friends' as possible ❏
b) To keep in touch with friends ❏
c) To meet new people ❏
d) To further my career ❏

8. How private/secure do you think your site is?
a) Entirely confidential ❏
b) Confidential and safe within my network ❏
c) Accessible by those who are 'friends' of 'friends' ❏
d) Entirely open to people I don't know ❏

9. **Has your life been enhanced by your social network?**
   a) Without doubt ☐
   b) To some extent ☐
   c) Hardly at all ☐
   d) Not at all ☐

10. **How often to you accept connecting invitations?**
    a) Always ☐
    b) Sometimes – depending on whether I know them ☐
    c) Infrequently – I keep my social network exclusive ☐
    d) Never ☐

SUNDAY

MONDAY

TUESDAY

WEDNESDAY

THURSDAY

FRIDAY

SATURDAY

Simple steps to networking success

Throughout this book, we have given you a framework for understanding networks and networking. We began by looking at definitions and identifying themes. All commentators agree that networks are built on contacts; contacts at all levels: personal, professional, within organizations and between organizations – virtual as well as real. Whatever the level of the contact and the aim in establishing it, the overriding goal of networking is to build and manage productive relationships.

The primary responsibility for your network lies with you!

Today, we will help you take on this responsibility by summarizing the book's activities, reiterating some of the most important aspects of good networking and suggesting some good habits to form.

For today, we have broken this down into five simple steps, which we cover in this chapter:

- Step one: Map your network
- Step two: Identify your style
- Step three: Clarify your goals
- Step four: Develop networking behaviours
- Step five: Benefit

Step one: Map your network

We live and work within networks, yet most people are unaware of them. If this lack of awareness persists, it will undermine the full effectiveness of managers in the future. Working with, through and in harmony with networks is a necessary skill if managers are to become successful and fulfil their potential. The first step to success requires that you understand who is in your network and where its strengths and weaknesses lie.

Network? What network?

You need to own and recognize your network. The most powerful way to understand your network is to see it. If you are on a professional website, you will be able to do this easily by clicking on your list of connections. Having done this, you will see a long list of people you are connected to and the type of relationship they have with you. You will also be able to see the latest activity on your site. However, you may prefer to map out your network to examine the different aspects and dynamics of it. Here's one method of doing so:

1 Take a piece of flipchart paper (anything smaller will be too small) and an ordinary pen (anything larger will be too large) and draw a circle in the middle of the paper with your name in it.
2 Draw a line to this circle. It will look like a lollipop.
3 At the end of this line, draw another circle. It will now look like a set of dumbbells.
4 Put the name of one of your primary networks in it – professional, personal, organizational, family...

5 Add more such lines until you have what looks like a daisy.
6 For each circle in your network tree, add more 'lollipops', into which you put the name and access information for your contact.
7 If one of your contacts was given to you by another member of your network and you haven't integrated them fully through building a personal relationship with them, connect them with a dotted line. Indicate the strength of your other relationships by thickening the lines between you and them.
8 Note the overlaps and gaps in your different networks and examine these in respect of your networking goals.

Don't be too fussy about how your map develops. Nobody else needs to understand it.

When you have completed your map with as many names as you can, stand back and look at it. Who have you forgotten? In Chapter 1, we gave you a list of potential network contacts. Have you included friends and acquaintances; family; school friends and teachers; college friends and academics; community leaders; church, parish and religious leaders; doctors and dentists; sports leisure or social club members; members of civic associations; former employers; colleagues and bosses from previous organizations; customers, suppliers, contractors, competitors, agents and distributors? Add any of these omissions to your map.

Your map will be constantly changing in accordance with your needs, goals, exposure and experiences.

Support your map with information. There are a number of computer packages that help you to organize the information you hold on people. Customer Relationship Management systems allow you to follow the trail of your communications with prospective clients and customers and record the content of your communication and prompts for the future. They will also remind you to make further contact at specific times. It is helpful to keep snippets of informal information on your records too. It is such an advantage to be able to open your conversation with a question such as:

How's your daughter doing at university?
Was your trip to Europe a success?
How did the bid presentation go?

or some other uncontentious question. Always keep your records up to date and in a format that enables you to update them easily.

Step two: Identify your style

Your map is a tangible illustration of where you have made your investment. To balance this picture, you need to reflect on your style. Attempt to answer the following question honestly:

What is your networking style?

You may need to look to the past to give yourself an indication of your style. *Do you:*

- like meeting new people?
- feel happiest focussed on a task or in a group?
- take opportunities to move in new circles?
- create opportunities to enhance your visibility or reputation?
- develop contacts in a wide variety of groups?
- stay in close contact with your customers or clients?
- enjoy meetings, training courses and conferences?
- know and talk to peers in other organizations?

Your answers to these questions will give you clues about your preferred style.

Remember from Chapter 1, there are three networking styles: conscious, intuitive and open.

- Conscious networkers have clear goals; they recognize the gaps in their network and identify opportunities to explore and find the people to fill the gaps.
- Intuitive networkers feel happiest when they are surrounded by people. They find themselves networking with everyone from their postman to other parents at the school gates.
- Open networkers invest in networks for their future potential. Translating such a network into something that is focussed and can deliver the goods may be a stumbling block for open networkers.

Networking isn't something that everyone feels comfortable
with immediately. If the thought of being surrounded by
people brings you out in a cold sweat, fills you with dread or
immediately raises your anxiety level, you need to develop your
skills consciously through scripting, rehearsing and practising.
It is not necessarily true that you don't have the ability to
network. You have probably never had the chance to practise
and develop your skills.

Step three: Clarify your goals

The planning is now complete for your journey. However, to
be a successful networker you need to have a destination in
mind. Once you have established your destination, it is easier
to monitor your progress as you journey along your route.
This requires action: establishing, maintaining, nurturing and
pruning your network.

What is your destination?

We introduced models in Chapter 1, which we have referred to
throughout the book. Networks are for:

● information
● development
● support
● influence.

Information

Managers need to keep up to date. To do this, a large amount of personal commitment, time and energy is required. To help you in this process, you need access to hubs and informers:

- Hubs:
  - are influential sources of information
  - suggest helpful connections.
- Informers:
  - provide new approaches and perspectives
  - recognize problems and opportunities
  - understand market trends and developments.

Be sure to choose your people well. Ensure that you consult with a variety of sources to get a balanced picture.

Development

A manager who isn't developing isn't performing. Continuous professional development (CPD) is now a pursuit expected of all professionals, based on the assumption that development isn't solely gained through initial training. You develop in many other ways: meetings, new projects, visits, seminars and reviews. The key to learning is reflecting on your experiences and making yourself conscious of the value you've taken from them and the skills you've developed as a result of them. It is important to keep asking yourself 'How could I improve?' You should also ask this of others who will be able to give you valuable feedback. Approach:

- Experts
  - those who are respected and valued
  - the people you would recommend to others.
- Challengers
  - cause you to look at your chosen direction
  - ask key questions about your life.

Seeking and receiving feedback openly and regularly creates a natural environment for development.

Support

No manger is an island! You need people to support you and to sponsor your entry into new networks. This will enable you to maintain and develop your networks. Ask yourself, 'Who should I surround myself with?'

- Foundations
  - on whom we depend.
- Sounding boards
  - hold you in the highest esteem
  - give you time.
- Guides
  - help you achieve your objectives
  - offer practical help and support.

Never underestimate the value of support. It can often go unrecognized until it's removed.

Influence

All managers need help along the way – people who can make things happen, endorse a project, open doors and offer you career guidance. Don't restrict yourself to just one person. Seek influential people within your organization or your profession. Ask yourself, 'Who could help me in the short and long term?'

- Resourcers
  - support you with resources
  - believe in your ideas.
- Mentors
  - guide your career
  - teach you the ropes.
- Promoters
  - advise you of opportunities
  - assist in enhancing your visibility.

Don't be afraid to ask. It can be flattering to be asked to fulfil an influencing role. People can always say no!

Planning your route

In planning your route, you first have to refer to your map. Are there any roadblocks? Do you have restricted access to information, development, support or influence?

Asking yourself this question will give you an indication of where you need to:

● invest
● hold
● prune.

Invest

Which relationships warrant investment currently? Which networks have you neglected recently?

● Personal
● Organizational
● Professional
● Social and professional websites

Which network could help you achieve your goals? If you have already decided what you want to achieve, you can probably identify the person who can help or support you in your endeavours. If this person is not immediately identifiable, think of how you might write a job advertisement specifying the type of person who could do it. You may recognize them as being inside one of your networks already.

You may decide to invest in the networks that you want to maintain or you may have identified gaps in your network that are critical.

Who could bridge the gap?

It is these issues that require investment.

Hold

You may have networks that, while important, require little special attention or effort. These are the networks that you can access at any point and personal investment is not always necessary. It could be that they are well developed or that others within them maintain them on your behalf – the family is a good example of this.

Prune

Which networks aren't so critical or important? You could choose to spend less time and energy on these. Decisions to prune networks are always difficult and can seem callous and calculating.

To have the energy to invest in new networks, you need to be realistic about those that are not serving you well and, where necessary, withdraw from them. You may need to prune people who are leaning too heavily on your good will and unable to repay you in a like manner.

Too many plans fail because the goal is not clear. Be clear in your goals and plan your route towards them. Always remember that plans may need to change as your circumstances change.

Regularly review your progress by asking yourself:

What do I want from my network?
What am I prepared to contribute to those in my network?

Your answers will keep you on the road to success.

Telling somebody about your plan is a good way of making your plan into a contract and ensuring that you stick to it. Also, hearing yourself saying things out loud and seeing others' reactions to what you're saying brings a new understanding and clarity. Choose your sounding boards with care. You could do so on the basis of their experience, skills and the quality of your relationship. This is a great way to start developing your networking skills and behaviours.

Step four: Develop networking behaviours

There is an unwritten code of ethics that ensures good networking practice.

Networking behaviours include the following:

- Be open-minded.
- Keep commitments.
- Treat others as you would like to be treated.
- Don't be afraid to ask.
- Give without expectation of a return.
- Say thank you.

Many people are cynical about networking as an activity. They see it as taking advantage of people's goodwill for personal gain. This is not the case. We all have a natural sense of justice. Try to gauge what this is for each person you contact. People will not co-operate if they feel that there is nothing in it for them – or not for very long, anyway. They very quickly get tired of giving and will soon stop. Networking, therefore, contains its own control system.

The best approach is 'treat others as you would like to be treated'. In this way, you can put yourself in the other person's shoes and ask whether your demands are reasonable. If you think you are stretching your credibility a bit, you might like to think of what incentives or rewards would balance the books.

Remember you are part of others' networks too so:

- Keep your eyes and ears open.
- Open doors for others.
- Refer and recommend people.
- Publicize others' achievements.
- Suggest projects or opportunities that will enhance their standing.

Step five: Benefit

Networking is here to stay. So, if you want to:

● ensure balance
● create visibility
● increase employability

understand and invest in your networks.

Ensure balance

Balance is hard to maintain. This is particularly true in current times because of the complex dynamics of life and the overlaps in our activities that we experience – such as the blurring of work and home. Nevertheless, networks can help you strike a balance between opposing forces in the following ways:

Balance
Support – Challenge
Doing – Thinking
Personal – Professional

By constantly monitoring and managing your networks, you can ensure that you reach a state of equilibrium.

Create visibility

Many large organizations today (especially flat or networked organizations) can be very impersonal. It is easy to get lost in the crowd. If you know how to network and how to identify the hubs and sponsors, people will get to know you.

Outside your organization, networks are fascinating. Once you begin networking, you will realize what a small world it is.

Increase employability

You can ensure your continued employability by:

● building networks with integrity
● bridging the gaps.

Building networks with integrity

Prospective employers may be interested in you solely because of your network. Professionals such as brokers, advertisers, salespeople, editors and consultants generally have key contacts with whom they have developed strong relationships. Often these contacts offer their allegiance to the individual rather than the organization. Employers may judge you on the quality and loyalty of your network. But be aware of contractual restrictions on using your network after leaving your organization.

Bridging the gaps

Successful people know that the way to good opportunities and advancement can come from a network that is carefully maintained. Make sure that you keep your network watertight by plugging the gaps with good 'bridging' relationships.

Summary

To do anything well requires focussed attention and effort. Networking is no exception. Throughout this week, we have been your companion in looking at how best to create and develop your network to advantage. We've encouraged you to think strategically about the purpose of your network, the people in it and your style of networking. Importantly, too, we asked you to think about the reciprocal nature of good networking practice. Small favours demonstrate that you're attentive to others and really do build goodwill.

Developing your network is not something to be done haphazardly. Your time is far too valuable to be wasted that way.

Know, develop and mobilize your network.

You will then be able to enjoy the rewards.

Networking is a highly valuable activity. It holds rewards for all parties if managed conscientiously. Have fun with your networks but use them wisely. With your 'networking eyes', you will see life's possibilities in a new light.

SUNDAY
MONDAY
TUESDAY
WEDNESDAY
THURSDAY
FRIDAY
SATURDAY

Questions

Answer the following questions honestly, reflecting on your networking skills.

1. **What is your natural networking environment?**
   a) I feel happiest in organizational groups ❑
   b) I look for opportunities to move into new circles ❑
   c) I network when my work depends on it ❑
   d) I don't seek or enjoy networking environments ❑

2. **If others were to describe your main networking characteristic, what would it be?**
   a) I tend to be the hub of others' networks ❑
   b) I am generally approached for the information I hold ❑
   c) I am known as a mentor or sponsor for others ❑
   d) I am not visible in others' networks ❑

3. **How do you use your networks?**
   a) For gathering information ❑
   b) For my personal development ❑
   c) For gaining support for my ideas and career ❑
   d) To access those who can influence on my behalf ❑

4. **If you were to describe your networking style, what would it be?**
   a) I think about and plan my networks ❑
   b) I build relationships naturally ❑
   c) I am conscious about my future needs and seed relationships early ❑
   d) I don't have a dominant style ❑

5. **How do you manage your networks?**
   a) I hold on to those who are important to me ❑
   b) I prune those contacts that are no longer valuable ❑
   c) I invest in those that I feel will bring me value ❑
   d) I don't manage my networks at all ❑

6. **Who do your networks contain?**
   a) No one obviously of benefit ❑
   b) Those who mentor and guide you ❑
   c) Those who promote and sponsor you ❑
   d) Those who build your reputation and visibility ❑

7. **In terms of support, does your network contain:**
a) A foundation – a touchstone on whom you can depend? ☐
b) A sounding board – for bouncing ideas off? ☐
c) A guide – to counsel you? ☐
d) A practitioner – who gives you practical assistance? ☐

8. **Which is the dominant function your network serves?**
a) Being supportive while acting as a challenge ☐
b) Giving you feedback on what you do ☐
c) Maintaining a healthy work/life balance ☐
d) My network doesn't assist me in finding balance ☐

9. **If you were to seek a new position, how ready is your network to assist you?**
a) I have the right people in my network and they are ready to assist me ☐
b) I have key contacts but need to build stronger relationships ☐
c) I need to plug a few gaps before I can use my network in this way ☐
d) My network cannot assist me in finding a new position ☐

10. **Looking forward, how equipped do you feel as a networker?**
a) I feel well equipped as a networker ☐
b) I now know what I need to do ☐
c) I need to build relationships with some key people as a minimum ☐
d) I still dread networking and will continue to avoid it! ☐

Surviving in tough times

In tough economic times, the futures of organizations and individuals can be unpredictable. So we'd suggest focussing on the things within your control – doing a great job, building an enviable reputation and creating strong networks that support you both personally and professionally. Reading this book will help you bring networking to life. Here are ten tips that, if applied, will help to strengthen your networking skills and your networks.

1 Understand your networks

Our networks evolve through association, and associations are developed through a variety of circumstances such as attending the same school or college, living in the same area or working in the same organization. In tough times the first step to networking success is to understand your network, who is in it, how it has grown and how you can develop it to benefit you.

2 Networks can benefit you!

Whether your networks exist for information, professional development, support or influence make sure that they benefit you. Mapping your network will give you some clues about how you have used your network in the past. For instance, you may have been very happy to ask for a recommendation, or for information, but you may have been the person that's supported others in their careers. Be conscious in your networking from this point on to ensure that your networks benefit you.

3 Start close to home!

Many people concentrate their efforts on their organizational networks, overlooking their personal network. We recommend that you start closer to home. Think about who is in your personal network, how it has developed and how it could be developed to support you. Remember that personal networks may benefit you professionally.

4 How well connected are you within your organization?

Being well connected in your organization is important in tough times. You obviously need to have a valuable skill set, a track record of achievement and authentic behaviours that support the values of the organization. However, without people in your professional network who know what you've achieved and the valuable contribution you've made, this can be lost. You need to challenge yourself to become your own advocate. Think about which projects would give you the highest profile and which people could be your greatest support – and connect with them.

5 Use professional networks

Professional networks are all about the connections you make and the potential they have to fuel your development. Often people are passive within their professional networks - receiving newsletters, attending events and conferences. However, you can use professional networks to your advantage. Use them to gain a platform, a profile or a valuable connection. Think about how your professional network can serve you best.

6 Think ahead

Networks are not just about today but tomorrow – you need to think ahead. In terms of your career you should be thinking about performance and perception. What do you want to achieve, what are others interested in and what will help you in the future? Most importantly, in terms of the future, you need to think of who will be able to support and develop you.

7 Use technology

Technology is a great tool if used correctly. Prospective employers will gather information about you from a variety of sources – so what impression will they get? Be clear about how technology can support your aim and be proactive in developing links and building your profile.

8 Develop networking behaviours

If you are not comfortable with networking then you need to start by giving yourself small challenges. Identify someone you want to connect with and think about how you might represent yourself in a meeting with them or attend an event you've always managed to avoid. If you are comfortable with networking then you need to develop your network to benefit you. This could be as simple as asking specific questions, or favours, of your network contacts.

9 Create visibility

Becoming visible is an important part of networking and this visibility can be in person or electronically. If you start with an end point in mind you should use all the resources available to you to create visibility. Comment on an event, write a blog, attend a seminar, ask a question, write a letter or just make contact with a colleague.

10 Keep reviewing your network

By their nature networks are dynamic, so do keep reviewing them. Be critical of the drain they put on you or the benefits they bring. Also review your networking skills – what works for you and what feels clumsy and needs further development. Don't review once; set a date with yourself at least every six months to review your networking and networks. In this way you can take control and it will reap untold rewards.

Notes

ALSO AVAILABLE IN THE 'IN A WEEK' SERIES

BODY LANGUAGE FOR MANAGEMENT ● BOOKKEEPING AND ACCOUNTING ● CUSTOMER CARE ● SPEED READING ● DEALING WITH DIFFICULT PEOPLE ● EMOTIONAL INTELLIGENCE ● FINANCE FOR NON-FINANCIAL MANAGERS ● INTRODUCING MANAGEMENT ● MANAGING YOUR BOSS ● MARKET RESEARCH ● NEURO-LINGUISTIC PROGRAMMING ● OUTSTANDING CREATIVITY ● PLANNING YOUR CAREER ● SUCCEEDING AT INTERVIEWS ● SUCCESSFUL APPRAISALS ● SUCCESSFUL ASSERTIVENESS ● SUCCESSFUL BUSINESS PLANS ● SUCCESSFUL CHANGE MANAGEMENT ● SUCCESSFUL COACHING ● SUCCESSFUL COPYWRITING ● SUCCESSFUL CVS ● SUCCESSFUL INTERVIEWING

For information about other titles in the series, please visit www.inaweek.co.uk

ALSO AVAILABLE IN THE 'IN A WEEK' SERIES

For information about other titles
in the series, please visit
www.inaweek.co.uk